THE FIRST BATTLE OF THE SEXES

BRIAN HUMPHREYS

THE FIRST BATTLE OF THE SEXES

Published in 2022 by FeedARead.com Publishing

First Edition

A CIP catalogue record for this title is available from the British Library.

Cover and all illustrations by Brian Humphreys

FOREWORD

According to scripture, Adam was created first and given three tasks: to tend the garden, to name the animals and to find himself a helper. What if the first animal he encountered was a dog that became his BFFF (Best Furry Friend Forever)?

Suppose Adam had the time of his life exploring the Garden of Eden for a day or two with his dog, doing whatever he wanted when he wanted, until the creator removed one of his ribs and created Eve, quicker in thought and often more emotional than Adam. Does that sound like a recipe for harmony?

Adam and Eve did not have Google or reference books to show them how to be fruitful and multiply, only newly-formed brains. Adam knew he had tadpoles to share with Eve but did not know how, and Eve thought she would have to lay an egg, and when she saw an ostrich egg, a painfully large ostrich egg, she vowed to remain a virgin forever.

3

Despite encouragement from the creator which created a few near-miss encounters, creation had stalled, leaving the creator only one option. He had to give his children the talk all parents dread - you know the one – the one about the birds and the bees.

With over 250 cartoon illustrations, please enjoy this humorous account of what might have happened in the Garden of Eden.

N.B. All profits from this humorous tale will be donated to help the work of **Kenya Hope Charity.**

KENYA HOPE CHARITY Reg.No.1173487

Responding to God's call to care for the poor

Please visit www.kenyahopecharity.org for details of their work with poor Kenyan orphans and widows.

CONTENTS

Page

CHAPTER 1

IN THE BEGINNING, THERE WAS MAN

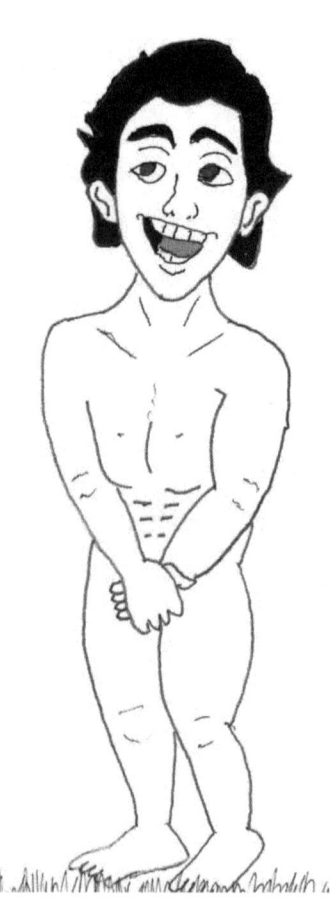

THE FIRST BATTLE OF THE SEXES

The newly-formed man felt a warm breeze move over his naked body as he sat up and opened his eyes and his eyes sparkled as details of his surroundings sharpened around him. He struggled to his feet and stared at the blue expanse above him.

'That's the sky, created by me on the second day,' said a voice, *'and the white lights are stars that I created on the fourth day.'*

The man plucked up a straight sturdy stick and tried to knock the stars out of the sky, much to the amusement of the creator.

'And the shimmering star that you are now looking at is the sun.'

The man turned his head from left to right in search of the creator until a symphony of birdsong attracted his attention.

The creator's voice was gentle and soothing. *'They are birds of every kind, I created them on the fifth day; don't they sound wonderful?'* The man dropped the stick and nodded in agreement as the gentle voice continued, *'And to you, I have given the gift of speech.'*

Instinctively, the man opened his mouth and spoke in a deep rich voice. 'Who am I?'

THE FIRST BATTLE OF THE SEXES

'You are man. I made you from dust and breathed life into you.'

'And where am I?'

'In the Garden of Eden.'

'This must be my first day for I cannot remember another.'

'That's right; this is indeed your first day and to you I have given the name Adam.' The creator looked over everything he had made and saw that it was good.

Adam flexed his arms and bent his legs. 'And what is my purpose?'

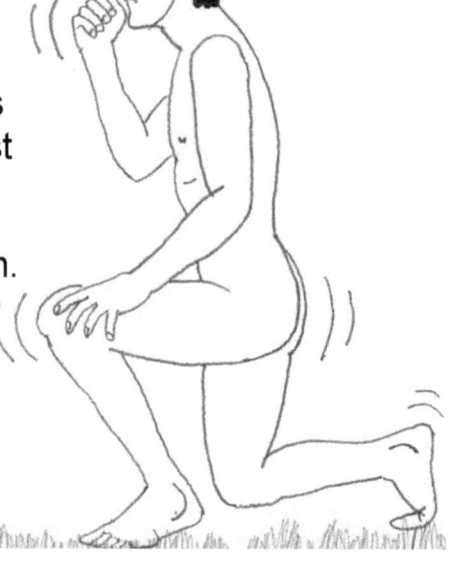

'To tend the garden,' said the creator, happy that his plan was working out just fine.

Adam looked about him. The garden stretched as far as his eyes could see. 'I don't really fancy manual work. Is there something else that I can do, I would hate to miss my potential?'

A heavenly sigh breathed down on Adam, ruffling his black curly hair. *'I need a gardener, take it or leave it.'*

'Will I have to wear a uniform?'

'There is no uniform, and I have given you dominion over all creatures.'

'Dominion? What's dominion?'

'It means that you're in charge, and your first task is to name the animals.'

Adam could see animals high in the trees and low to the ground, close by and in the distance and in every direction. 'You want me to name *all of them,* by myself?'

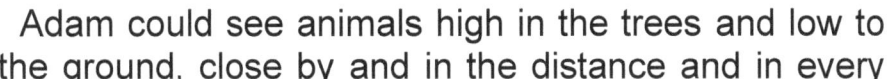

'Inside the head that you're scratching,' explained the creator, *'is a brain. If you use it, it will help you to find a helper.'*

Adam rubbed his chin. 'That's still a lot of work, even with a helper, and do I have to start right now?'

The creator's smile began to fade. *'I suppose it can wait; after all, I have given you free will.'*

'Free will?'

'It means that you can start now, or later.'

Adam grinned. 'I like the sound of free will. I'll start tomorrow because I have a large garden to explore.'

The creator's voice took on a more serious tone. *'The Garden of Eden is full of trees, bushes and shrubs that are pleasing to the eye and good for food. You can eat anything you like, except from the tree with the forbidden fruit.'*

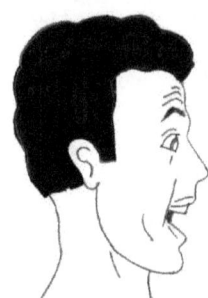

Adam jumped up and down. 'A tree with forbidden fruit? Where? Where is it?'

'It's over there,' said the creator, wondering why he hadn't stopped after making the elephants, *'on the tree of the knowledge of good and evil.'*

'And what happens if I eat the forbidden fruit?'

'Fear of the Lord,' cried a thunderous voice from the clouds, *'is the beginning of wisdom. Do not eat from the tree of the knowledge of good and evil because if you do, you will surely die.'* Lightning bolts quickly followed and scratched the clear blue sky.

Adam, who had fallen over at the sound of thunder and the flash of lightning dusted himself down. 'OK, there's no need to get your lightning bolts in a twist!'

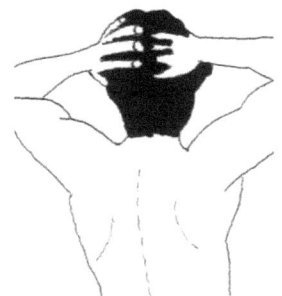

With the warmth of the sun caressing his face, Adam flexed his arms, stood up and took his first tentative step, inhaling powerful aromas as he moved unsteadily towards nearby trees, their knotted branches rising ever upwards as far as his head could lift. Birds flitted in and out of the trees singing their beautiful melodies and a gentle breeze shuffled overhead leaves. A brown furry animal swung into the trees and branches creaked in protest. A word came into Adam's mind: monkey.

'Ooh, ooh, aah,' chattered the monkey.

'Ooh, ooh, aah,' copied Adam before climbing the trees to see the monkey more clearly. Soon he was three branches high. Using vines, the monkey swung into the adjacent tree that had large green leaves and bunches of yellow fruit. Not to be outdone, Adam grabbed a vine and swung after him, but the vine snapped under his weight and his body landed with a thud in a mossy hollow.

'I guess I'm not designed to swing through trees,' he declared, enjoying once again the sound of his deep voice.

11

The monkey swung to another branch dislodging a yellow fruit that fell at Adam's feet. After inspecting the fruit, Adam decided that it was a banana and he could eat it. He sank his teeth into the yellow skin. 'Urgh,' he moaned spitting the yellow skin onto the ground, 'I don't think much of bananas.'

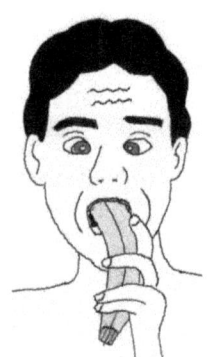

Knowing that it was only a matter of time before Adam would take everything in his stride, the creator looked on with amusement.

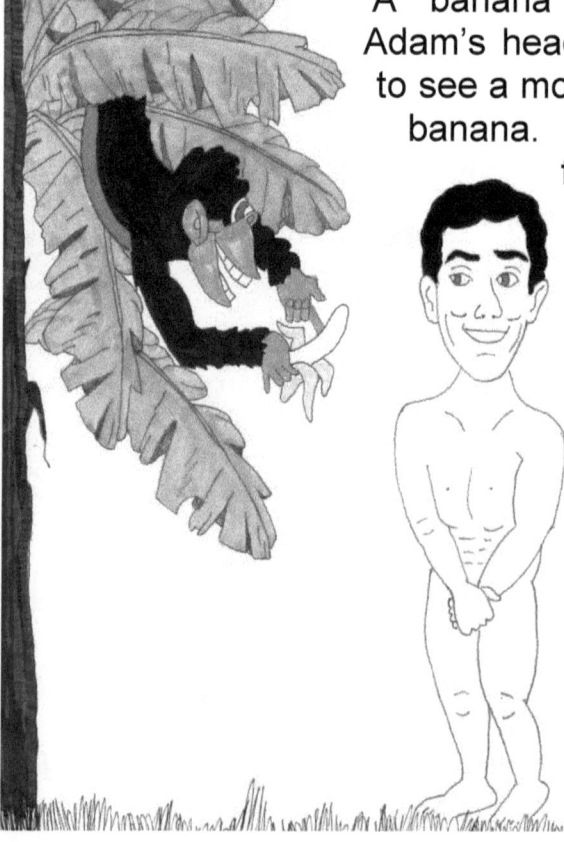

A banana skin bounced off Adam's head and he looked up to see a monkey peel and eat a banana. Plucking a banana from the tree, Adam peeled it and ate the white inner fruit. 'Now that's more like it,' he said, licking his lips. Adam began to collect more bananas but every time he turned to pick another one, monkeys stole some from his pile.

Sensing that food would be plentiful wherever he roamed, Adam moved away from the fruit trees to explore a new sound. 'This is a river,' Adam declared, looking proudly at his third discovery of the day. The low sun bounced off the rippling surface creating flashes of colour and movement as Adam carefully lowered himself into the water until his feet touched the bottom. The cold water sent 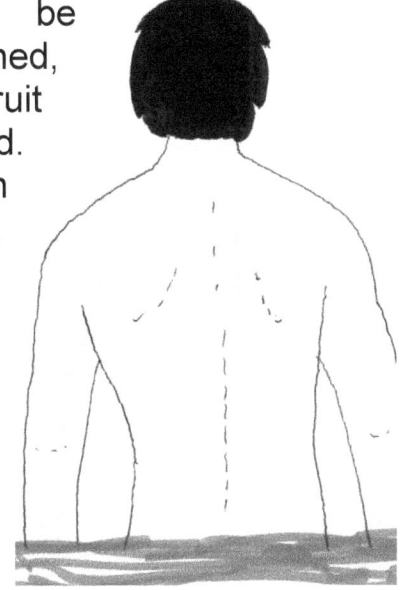 shivers through him as he washed his hair and washed the dust from his body. He cupped water into his hands and enjoyed the taste of the cold liquid before returning to land to dry off in the soothing warmth of the setting sun. Many animals came to the river to drink, but Adam, too tired to begin the task of naming them, moved to a more sheltered place to lay his weary head.

On that first evening, Adam studied the sky and wondered for some time as to why the sun shone; and then it dawned on him.

CHAPTER 2

MAN FINDS A HELPER

THE FIRST BATTLE OF THE SEXES

With eyes closed, Adam relaxed in the warmth of the morning sunshine until a rough wet tongue rasped across his cheek. His eyes snapped fully open and he jumped to his feet, his new and perfect world spinning wildly about him. 'Who am I? Where am I? And what is my purpose?'

'Have you forgotten already?' boomed the voice from above. *'You are Adam, you are in the Garden of Eden, and your first task is to name the animals.'*

Both Adam and a creature with a furiously wagging tail searched the sky for the source of the voice. Adam patted the creature on the head. 'You are warm blooded and covered with fur. Can you talk?' The creature barked and the noise sent a flock of birds skimming through the sky above. Adam looked up, 'excuse me Mr Creator, is this a dog?'

The creator filled the clear blue sky with a beautifully coloured arch of shimmering in- candescent colours. *'Hallelujah, at last you have begun to use your brain.'*

15

THE FIRST BATTLE OF THE SEXES

In the far distance beneath the rainbow, Adam could see a great sweep of land with blue-topped mountains, in the middle distance he could see livestock and wild animals grazing peacefully together, and in front of him sat the friendliest animal he had so far encountered. 'Come on,' Adam urged the dog, 'we've got a whole new world to explore.'

'And don't forget to name the animals,' reminded the creator.

Adam searched the sky once more. 'I've already named a monkey and a dog, give me a chance.'

'And don't eat the fruit from the tree of the knowledge of good and evil,' shouted the creator.

The dog looked around nervously until Adam explained, 'Relax, that's the creator and he's given us free will which means that we can do whatever we like. Race you to that tree. Go!' Despite Adam leading from the start, the dog easily reached the tree first, cocked his leg, and sprayed the tree trunk with scent. Gasping for breath, Adam soon caught up with his dog and did the same. The dog sniffed Adam's scent which Adam felt was a little strange as he had no urge to sniff the dog's scent. 'My little friend, because you have a white patch on your head, I think I'll call you Patch.'

The dog raised two front paws in the air and Adam smacked one, completing the world's first high-five. 'Patch it is then.' Patch sat back, leaned slightly to one side, put his head between his legs and began to lick and clean himself. Deciding to copy his dog, Adam sat down and also tried to lick himself clean, but gambolled backwards into a bed of pansies.

'Ooh, ooh, aah,' came the sound from high in the banana trees as Adam plucked squashed pansies from his hair. Panting in a steady rhythm, Patch placed both front paws against the tree trunk and fixed his eyes on the brown furry creature above.

Doubting that his dog would have the ability to climb trees, Adam gave Patch an order. 'Stay! They're monkeys, I learned about them yesterday.' A banana fell to the ground and Patch pushed it around with his nose, sniffing it inquisitively. Adam picked up the banana and Patch sat before him, willing him to throw it.

'This is not a toy,' explained Adam, trying to impress his new best friend. 'It's food; watch this.' Adam peeled back the yellow skin and broke off a piece of the inner white fruit. 'Catch!' Patch caught and swallowed the piece of banana and begged for more. 'Come on,' said Adam revelling in his position of master, 'I want to show you something else.'

At the river, Adam lowered his body into the water. 'This is a river, I discovered it yesterday.' With no intention of getting wet, Patch remained on solid ground watching curiously. Adam washed himself down and began to examine the smooth white texture of his skin, the faint blue lines beneath suggesting veins, his large powerful chest muscles, the deep hollow down the centre of the back, the bony ridges of the spine, the black hair growing on his chest, under his arms, and around his dangly thing. He dug his fingers into his chest and began counting bones. 'Hey, Patch, I've got twelve pairs of ribs.'

Patch wagged his tail. If his master was happy, he was happy.

Enticed by the flashing silver of quick-moving creatures below the surface, Adam ducked underwater to investigate and learned another valuable lesson: when underwater, close your mouth. He lifted his head and spat out a mouthful of water and three small fish. More interested in taking a nap, Patch walked in a circle several times to flatten some grass and settled down into his self-made bed. That's one clever dog, Adam decided.

Seated by the river, Adam began the task of naming the animals as they came to drink. A long-necked animal with long spindly legs lowered its head into the water. 'I name you giraffe,' said Adam. 'Can you talk? Would you like to be my new helper?' With no answer forthcoming, Adam turned to see a large grey animal with legs as thick as tree trunks stomp its way to the river. 'You are an elephant and your funny long nose is called a trunk. Can you talk?' The elephant sucked water into its trunk and squirted him. Adam shook his mop of black hair and wiped his face. 'I'll take that as a no then.'

More animals came to the river and Adam named tigers, gazelles, lions and lambs; animals so different, yet living in harmony. After naming zebras, cattle, sheep, pigs, goats and polar bears, Adam became bored. None of the animals could speak, how on earth could they become his helper?

Tired and weary, Adam turned to his dog. 'I'm not searching for a new helper any more, the job's yours.'

Adam lived in a perfect world with a perfect companion and he was in charge. Creation, he decided, was just perfect.

The sky to the east still offered defiant rays of late sun as the creator put the man into a deep, deep, sleep; and during the night, Adam experienced his first bad dream: that someone was stealing one of his ribs.

Waking underneath the leafy umbrella of a large tree with a sore chest and one rib missing came as a huge shock to Adam. He counted his sore ribs for a third time. One rib was definitely missing and this was a mystery that he intended to solve.

'PATCH!' Patch, his coat of black and white fur shining in the sunlight scampered towards his master anticipating a belly-rub but Adam ordered him to 'SIT!' The dog sat to attention, excited at this new game and ready to pounce on his master at the first opportunity, but Adam's frown kept Patch motionless. 'I've got a bone to pick with you.' The dog's ears stood to attention. This sounded promising.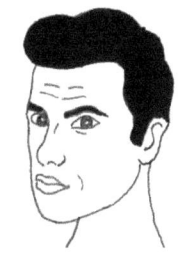

 'Did you take my rib?'

Patch wagged his tail.

'Or was it somebody else?'

Patch wagged his tail.

Deciding that it wasn't the work of his dog, Adam and Patch set off in search of an answer. 'Those monkeys stole some of my bananas a few days ago, let's question them.' At the banana trees, Adam announced his arrival with a loud call, 'ooh, ooh, aah.' A monkey appeared carrying a large bunch of bananas and Adam came straight to the point. 'Did you steal my rib?'

'Ooh, aah, aah,' said the monkey, climbing back into the trees.

A new noise caught Adam's attention.

'Pssssst,' hissed a strange creature whose dark eyes snapped open to reveal red pupils as bright as marbles as it hung down from a tree.

Adam studied the creature, amazed to hear another voice, albeit a strange hissing voice. 'You're a snake, I can tell by your covering of shiny green scales, and you can talk.'

'That'sss right,' hissed the snake dropping an apple at Adam's feet. Why don't you tassste thisss apple? It'sss sso much sssweeter than a banana.' The snake's head thrust forward, its forked tongue dancing hypnotically, its eyes a-glitter with evil. 'Jussst try one sssmall bite, then I'll tell you who ssstole your rib.'

Before Adam could pick up the apple, Patch decided that his master was in danger and charged, sending the snake scurrying out of sight.

'BAD DOG!' shouted Adam. 'You've scared away the only talking creature. Now I'll never know what happened to my rib.'

CHAPTER 3

AND THEN THERE WERE TWO

With Patch following behind him, Adam headed to the river in the hope that a shower might ease the pain of his sore chest and take his mind off his missing rib. On the way, he noticed a new pale-skinned creature peeping out from behind a bush.

Under watchful eyes, Adam named camels, pigs, unicorns, woolly mammoths and velociraptors. Wading birds came next, and after naming a pink bird with skinny legs a flamingo, Adam shouted to Patch. 'Look! The creator's made a mistake, he's put the knees of the flamingo on back to front.'

A loud voice pierced the clouds, *'I HAVE NOT MADE A MISTAKE!'*

At the sound of giggling, Adam spun around to see the new creature with yellow hair laughing at him from behind a bush. In an effort to impress, Adam continued to name the procession of animals as quickly as he could but hesitated over a strange bird with a large beak.

'That's a dodo,' the new creature said.

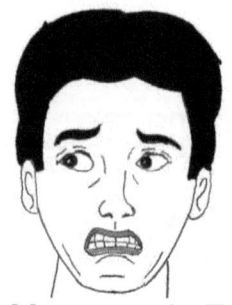

'It's my job to name the animals,' Adam pointed out. 'I was created first.'

'Yes, you were,' the new creature said gaining confidence, 'but then God stood back and said to himself, "I can do better than that", and he created me. My name is Eve.'

Adam puffed out his chest. 'Hold it right there, it's my job to give out names. I think I'll call you Olive.'

The new creature emerged from behind a bush and folded her arms. 'An olive is a fruit. I am a woman, made by the creator from your rib to be your equal. I was *not* made from your foot to be trodden on.' Adam clenched and un-clenched his fists. Olive wasn't acting like an equal, more like a superior, and had far too much to say for herself. 'I'm here to help you,' she continued, 'whether you like it or not!'

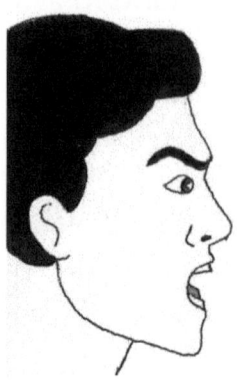

Adam did not like it. He did not like it one bit. 'Do you always have to have the last word?'

'No.'

'There you are, you just did it again.'

'Didn't.'

Adam digested her comments in frustrated silence. This new creature was annoyingly quicker in thought. He decided to appeal to the heavens. 'Excuse me, creator, what's your exchange policy?'

The creator's voice pierced the clouds. *'There is no exchange policy!'*

With Patch by his side, Adam politely led Eve around the garden with a fixed smile on his face, resigned to sharing his once perfect world. 'This way, Olive, I've discovered a few things already.' Eve reluctantly followed him until he stopped. 'This,' he announced proudly, 'is a banana tree.'

Eve corrected him. 'That is not a banana *tree*, it's a banana *plant*;' and when two bananas fell at her feet, she picked them up. 'And these are bananas, food for us to eat.'

Adam acted as though he had never seen one before. 'If this is food, how on earth do we eat it?'

Exactly how they should be eaten she hadn't yet received the knowledge, but determined not to show weakness she said, 'We eat them like this,' and bit into the yellow skin and although it was bitter and tough, she continued to chew.

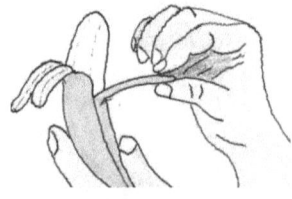

After a few moments, Adam peeled back the outer skin of his banana. 'I find it's best to eat them like this,' he said smugly.

Annoyed at being tricked, Eve threw down a challenge. 'You may have been created first, but show me one thing that you can do that I can't.'

Not one to shirk a challenge, Adam wrote his name in the sand using water from his dangly-thing. 'Bet you can't do that!' Immediately, Patch ran over for a sniff and ruined the world's first graffiti.

Embarrassed and no longer content to trail behind, Eve moved ahead of Adam and Patch to the river, and as she bent over to study more closely the small flashes of colour that moved quickly below the surface, she came face-to-face with her reflection. 'Thank goodness I'm not alone with him,' she said to the girl underwater. 'He's the most annoying man that I've ever met.'

Just out of earshot, Adam turned to his dog as they sat and watched her. 'Do you think that I should warn her to close her mouth when underwater?'

Patch wagged his tail.

'Or let her find out the hard way?'

Patch wagged his tail.

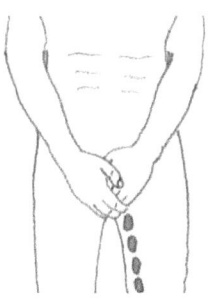

Eve leaned forward a little too far and her body entered the water with a splash, the twin ovals of her bottom sticking out above the surface. A few seconds later, she returned to an upright position and spat out some fish.

Adam laughed all the way to the bank. 'Are you OK?' he said, looking down on her with a grin that was three parts amusement and one part concern. 'That was so funny,' he continued, 'water came out of my dangly thing and ran down my leg.'

As Adam pulled her from the river, Eve could feel her face burning and the tears that followed were a welcome release from the stresses of her first day.

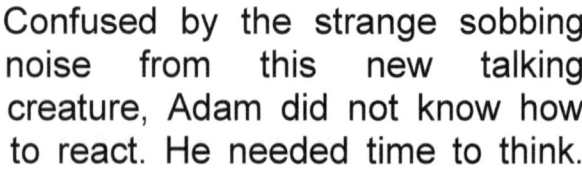

Confused by the strange sobbing noise from this new talking creature, Adam did not know how to react. He needed time to think. 'PATCH, HERE BOY!' he yelled. His faithful dog ran to his side and receiving a pat on the head for his loyalty. 'We'll be back later,' he said, 'we've got work to do.'

Eve dried her tears. 'How long before you come back?'

Adam shrugged. 'I can't tell.'

'You can tell me, I won't tell anyone.'

'I mean, I can't be sure.'

'Well, can't you take a guess?'

'Not until tomorrow.'

'You can't take a guess until tomorrow?'

A smile spread across Adam's face. 'Gotcha!'

Eve clenched her fists. 'That's not funny, Adam. How long will you be gone?'

'All of the time.'

With nothing nearby to throw, she made do with pulling a funny face at him.

In an effort to avoid thinking about Eve or his sore rib, Adam decided to build a man-cave. Wanting to be near to food, he chose to build it around the base of a banana tree, but how and with what? Patch appeared and dropped a small branch at Adam's feet. Patch sat patiently waiting for his master to throw it, but Adam inspected the branch thoughtfully. 'Where did you find this, Patch? Show me.'

Deciding that his master was not going to throw it, Patch ran back to the nearby wood to fetch another stick. Adam followed and found many branches that had been broken from trees, probably by elephants Adam decided as he stepped around large piles of animal droppings. He carried branches back to the banana tree and tried to stack them on top of each other to make walls, but they kept falling down. Adam's ever-improving brain gave him an idea and he returned to the trees that had vines. After finding a sharp stone, he cut some lengths of vine and returned to the banana tree. After several attempts, Adam constructed three walls around the base of the banana tree by tying the branches together with vines. After laying large banana leaves over it for the roof, he stood back to admire his new home. Scratched, bruised, and with sweat on his brow, Adam settled down inside, but Patch, his sixth sense telling him that it might collapse at any moment, chose to stay just outside.

Adam tried to justify his desertion of Eve. 'I know she's only a day old, but she will be OK on her own, won't she?'

Patch wagged his tail.

'Or should I go find her?'

Patch wagged his tail.

Annoyed that Adam did not care about her and her needs, Eve turned her attention to the beauty of her new world and minute-by-minute, all the creatures, sounds and colours grew in clarity. Quickly forgetting Adam, she skipped along behind butterflies, buzzing bees and whirring dragonflies until she found herself in a sunken meadow full of bluebells, yellow buttercups, red poppies and other flowers whose names so far eluded her. Surrounded by bright colours, she bathed in soft perfumes before dancing into another field.

As the sun began to disappear behind nearby hills, she leaned against a tiger and settled down to sleep, luxuriating in the softness of the fur and the warmth of the tiger's body. Although amongst tigers with teeth surely designed to grip and tear flesh apart and not designed to eat grass and leaves, she held no fear.

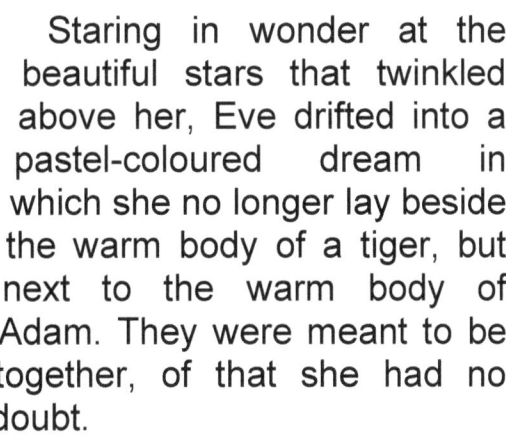

Every creature she had so far encountered lived in perfect harmony with no sign of argument or disagreement, except for one notable exception: the man with black hair, deep blue eyes and a muscular body.

Staring in wonder at the beautiful stars that twinkled above her, Eve drifted into a pastel-coloured dream in which she no longer lay beside the warm body of a tiger, but next to the warm body of Adam. They were meant to be together, of that she had no doubt.

33

THE FIRST BATTLE OF THE SEXES

In the semi-darkness of his man-cave, Adam lay on his back, so tired that his muscles complained, so tense that he could not drop off. Although his man-cave was empty, he was not alone. Eve's words and his own doubts crowded around him. Although drained of energy, the few moments of sleep took him into confused dreams. Sometimes, he saw himself in Eve's arms happy and contented but other times, they were face-to-face arguing. He couldn't work her out and it bothered him.

CHAPTER 4:

THE
ARGUMENTS
BEGIN

The morning sunrise was a breath-taking display of radiant colours with streaks of red, pink and orange slowly overcoming the dark blue of the twilight sky. The tigers had moved on and Eve was all alone. As the sun's brilliant rays warmed the air, she began to cry.

The creator's soothing voice slowed her tears. *'Eve; what on earth is the matter? The tigers are not far away, and isn't it a beautiful morning?'*

'Look, can't you see,' she sobbed, pointing overhead. 'All of the stars have fallen from the sky.'

'My dear Eve, I created the stars on the fourth day, and they will return every evening when the sun goes down.'

Eve calmed down. 'I remember my name and that I am a woman, but what is my purpose?'

'To help Adam.'

'Isn't there someone else that I can help?'

'There are just the two of you for now.'

Eve pounced on the creator's slip of the tongue. 'For now? You meant there are more people to come?'

'One day.'

'What do you mean, one day? Just how much longer am I stuck here all alone with bossy-boots?'

'All of the creatures that swim in water, fly in the sky or walk on the land are programmed to be fruitful and multiply, and so my dear are you. Your job is to populate the world.'

'All by myself? That sounds like a lot of hard work for just one woman.'

'Adam will help you; he is also programmed to populate the world.'

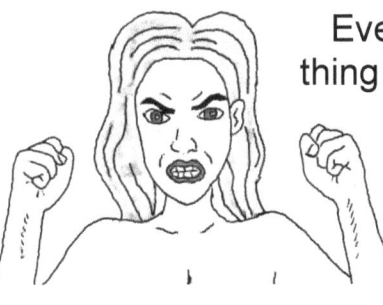

Eve clenched her hands, the last thing she wanted to do was to work with Adam unless he apologised for the way he had treated her. 'Well he can wait,' Eve shouted, setting off to gain more knowledge.

She turned her attention to a pair of birds happily chirping their song in a nearby bush. As she crept towards them, they flitted from their nest to reveal the reason for their joy. Eve peered inside at three eggs and excitement fizzed through her. Instinctively, she knew that the eggs represented new life. She stepped back, allowing the birds to once again sit on their eggs. That's to keep them warm, Eve realised.

Satisfied with a morning of new discoveries, Eve stretched out her naked body in the full glare of the sun and tried to forget about helping Adam to populate the world. In the dream that followed, Eve felt the warmth of Adam's body pressing down on hers and she braced herself, hoping that he would know what to do next, because she hadn't a clue.

Adam woke to the same beautiful sunrise as Eve, but it had done little to raise his spirits. He was not looking forward to sharing the Garden of Eden. Deciding to protest at the new arrangements, Adam chose his words carefully. 'Good morning, Mr Creator,' he began. 'Can I talk to you about that new creature that you made for me? We had words yesterday. Unfortunately, I didn't get to use mine.'

The creator chuckled.

Determined to make his point, Adam continued, 'I was having a perfectly wonderful existence until *she* arrived. Olive sees beauty in all of creation, except for me.'

The reply came loud and clear. *'HER NAME IS EVE!'* The blast of wind that followed the creator's voice reminded Adam that, although he'd been created first and given dominion over all creatures, he was *not* in charge of creation. Patch crouched low, shaking with fear, until the voice from above returned to its usual calm and loving tone. *'You will soon become friends with Eve. In fact, if you hurry, she's heading for the river.'*

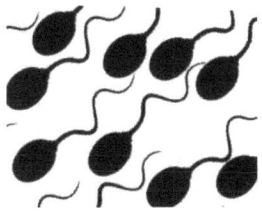

Attracted by the sound of frogs croaking, Adam discovered a tiny pond and watched with fascination as tiny black creatures wiggled just below the surface. 'You are tadpoles,' he told the small creatures, 'you are new life.'

Eve noticed Adam approaching as she washed in the cool sparkling water of the river, but continued to name and wash her body parts. Her special body part, the one through wish she assumed she would lay eggs one day, she washed last.

With Patch nowhere in sight, Adam eased himself into the water and moved to her side. If she was to become a permanent fixture in the Garden of Eden, Adam thought, her naked body would certainly brighten the place up. He splashed her with water. 'Has anyone ever told you how beautiful you are?'

Hope flamed inside Eve and she splashed him back. 'That was a nice thing to say.'

'Well it's true, you're almost as beautiful as my dog.' Adam massaged her shoulders, his warm breath caressing her neck.

It was the first time that she'd been touched by someone else, and she didn't know how to react. Her body wanted more but she decided to stop him.

'Take your hands off me.' Feeling confused and betrayed by her own body, Eve climbed out of the river with tears in her eyes. The tingling she had felt yet another mystery in the secret depths of her being.

Adam hauled himself out of the water. 'What have I done now? Stop crying, and act your age.'

She picked up and threw a coconut at his smiling arrogant face but missed him by several feet. 'I am acting my age, I'm two days old.'

Adam grinned. 'You even throw like a girl.'

'I'm not a girl, I'm a woman in case you haven't noticed.'

'Oh, I've noticed,' he said.

She threw a second coconut which hit Adam full on the chest. 'Gotcha, gotcha!' Eve shouted but her yells of triumph died in her throat when he collapsed to the ground holding his scar. She crouched over him. 'Are you OK Adam? Say something.'

After lying still for a few minutes, Adam stood up. 'Gotcha!' he shouted and pointed to his scar. 'You have absolutely no idea how much pain is involved in bringing another person into the world.'

Eve jumped to her feet, 'I can't believe you've tricked me *again*, you must think that I was born yesterday.'

'You were created yesterday from my rib, can I have it back?'

As Eve began to cry, Adam felt confused. He should be the one in control, but he clearly wasn't and he had no idea why she was crying.

'It's not you, it's me,' Eve conceded. 'I just thought that you might have wanted to do what the other animals are doing.'

Adam thought hard. 'What? Eating grass, climbing trees, running, swimming, laying eggs? At least, give me a clue.'

'It doesn't matter, just forget it,' sighed Eve, glad that he knew about eggs.

'How can I forget it if I didn't know what it was in the first place?'

Tired of yet another verbal battle, Eve decided not to ask him about helping her to populate the world; instead, she changed the subject. 'Why are your arms so scratched?'

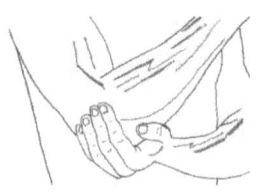

Adam bragged about his new man-cave. 'It all began when Patch dropped a stick at my feet.' Eve wondered if he could read her mind and knew that she was thinking of building a home for the two of them. 'So I gathered up branches and stacked them high, but they kept falling down, so I said to Patch, "At this rate, I'll never build us a home".'

Despite the realisation that when he said 'us', he meant his dog and not her, Eve watched the pulse beating strongly in his neck and discretely inhaled his manly scent. She wanted him to stop talking about his man-cave and his dog and to focus on her for a change but Adam was content to be close to her. If only she'd come

back to my place, he thought, telling her how he'd used vines to tie the branches together and used banana leaves for the roof.

This house must be worth seeing, she decided. 'Adam, I want you to take me.'

Adam did not need telling twice. Using his muscular arms, he swept her off her feet.

Eve screamed, kicking out wildly. 'What are you doing? Put me down!'

Adam dropped her to the floor. 'You quite clearly said, "I want you to take me."'

'I meant, take me to your new home.'

'Well how was I to know, I'm not a mind-reader? I thought you meant...' Adam's voice tailed off and Eve tried to make amends for not making herself clear because of new emotions that she didn't fully understand.

'Please don't go off on your own. I'm your new helper, can't I come with you?'

Adam decided to give her a second chance. 'All right, but on one condition, you do as I tell you because ...'

'Don't tell me, let me guess . . .' she interrupted, 'because you were created first?'

Patch appeared herding several sheep towards them and Adam asked him, 'why have you brought me some sheep?'

'It's because he's a sheepdog,' Eve pointed out . 'Don't you know anything?'

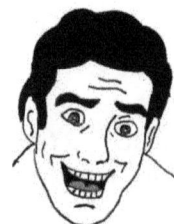

'I do know how to play hide and seek. You run and hide, I'll close my eyes and count to 100 and then I'll come and find you. One, two, three, four... go on, run and hide.'

Although not sure about this new game, Eve began to run away, but could sense Adam's eyes on her. 'Stop staring,' she shouted.

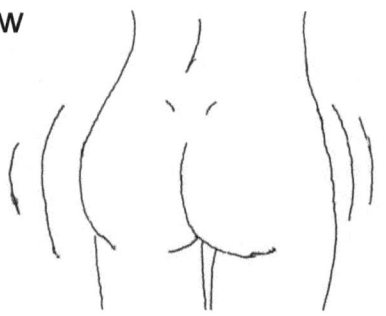

'I'm not,' grinned Adam continuing his count.

CHAPTER 5

THE FIRST SLEEPOVER

THE FIRST BATTLE OF THE SEXES

After peeping out from behind a tree a dozen times, Eve soon realised that she had been tricked by Adam again. Finding it difficult to push him to the back of her mind, Eve drew pictures in the loose earth with a pointed stick. If only she had something to draw on. Using a sharp stone, she cut some banana leaves roughly the same size and by using a porcupine quill to make holes, she carefully sewed the leaves together along one edge with pieces of vine creating the world's

first book. Next challenge, something to draw with. After experimenting with different pebbles and slates, Eve found one that would leave a mark on the leaves. Now she could draw. Her first effort was a sketch of Adam's face with his stupid grin. After hiding her face book she ate a banana.

'Pssst,' hissed a snake, appearing from inside the leaves of a nearby shrub. The snake raised its head, its green scales shimmered and shone and its forked tongue moved excitedly from side to side. 'Hello missss.'

Eve stared in fascination at the talking snake that hooded its eyes to disguise its evil intent. 'Hello Mr Snake, how are you?'

'Jussst sswell. Try thiss apple, it'ss much ssweeter than a banana.'

'An apple is 126 calories and contains very little vitamin C whereas bananas contain potassium, vitamin B and vitamin C, so I'll stick with bananas thank you.'

'Take jusst one bite, it'ss golden and deliciouss,' hissed the snake, 'and then I'll help you ssort out bossy-bootss once and for all.'

That was all the encouragement Eve needed. 'Now you're talking, give me that apple.'

Following the snake's strong scent, Patch ran around the corner growling loudly, and the hissing snake disappeared quickly into the undergrowth. Patch rubbed against Eve's legs and waiting for a reward or something to eat; and much to his delight she knelt down, patted him on the head and tickled his ear. Patch tried to lick her face but she pushed him away. 'I'm grateful, but not that grateful. Take me to bossy boots.' Patch tilted his head. 'Take me to the one who keeps saying, "I was created first".'

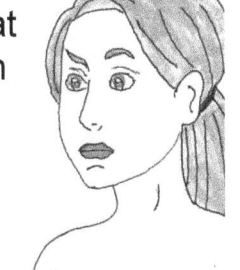

Now Patch understood and set off with Eve following close behind.

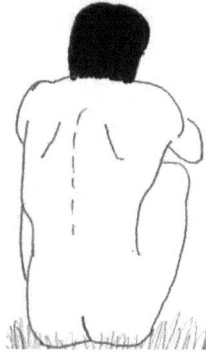

When she spotted Adam, Eve realised how much she had missed the company of another human. Her heartbeat increased as she neared him and the fact that he was sitting on the ground and his deep blue eyes were fixed on a chicken puzzled her. 'Adam, can I ask a silly question?'

'Better than anyone I know.'

'Why are you staring at that chicken?'

'You know everything Eve, so tell me, which do you think came first, the chicken or the egg?'

'Obviously the creator made the chicken and the chicken laid the egg. Answer me this, why do you think tigers have sharp teeth but only eat grass and flowers? Do you think they have sharp teeth so that they can kill and eat other animals?'

Adam shook his head. 'Of course not. Death doesn't exist so long as we don't eat forbidden fruit from the forbidden tree.'

Eve's eyes grew larger. 'Forbidden fruit, forbidden tree, where, where?'

Adam led her to the tree of the knowledge of good and evil. 'We mustn't eat from this tree, the creator told me personally.'

She shook her hair back from her face. 'I believe you, but thousands wouldn't.'

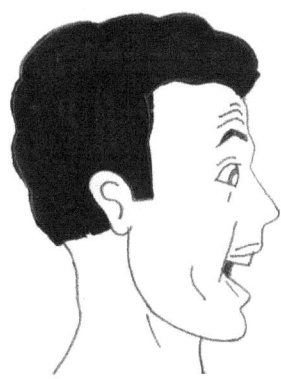

Adam decided that he needed to keep a closer eye on her. 'Would you like to spend the night with me?'

'What do you mean, "spend the night with you?"' she replied, her heart jumping at the thought of his muscular body keeping her warm at night.

'I'm tired, it's getting dark, and I'm going to my man-cave for a sleep. Would you like to come?'

Although her emotions were confused, his invitation comforted her, especially as her resistance of him seemed to be melting.

When they reached his man-cave, there were large holes in the banana leaf roof had and the floor was littered with monkey poo and banana skins. Adam tried to repair the roof and Eve began to sweep the man-cave clean using ostrich feathers.

THE FIRST BATTLE OF THE SEXES

'I can't believe you built your home under a banana plant with edible leaves for the roof, Adam; even I'm not that stupid.'

Adam considered reminding her about the game of hide-and-seek but she was doing such a good job with the housework he decided to keep quiet. With the roof patched up and housework finished, they lay down.

'Goodnight,' said Eve, thrilled at his nearness. The heat from Eve's body and the fact that she was within touching distance was having an effect on Adam. 'Sweet dreams,' whispered Eve, 'oh, and one more thing.' Adam wondered what this 'one more thing' might be. 'No funny business!' she added.

Eve lapsed into a sleep and dream that was anything but sweet. She had been filled with Adam's tadpoles and was pushing and pushing with all of her might. 'Keep going, you're almost there,' Adam shouted, and then she pushed out new life and yelled, 'Look Adam, our first egg.'

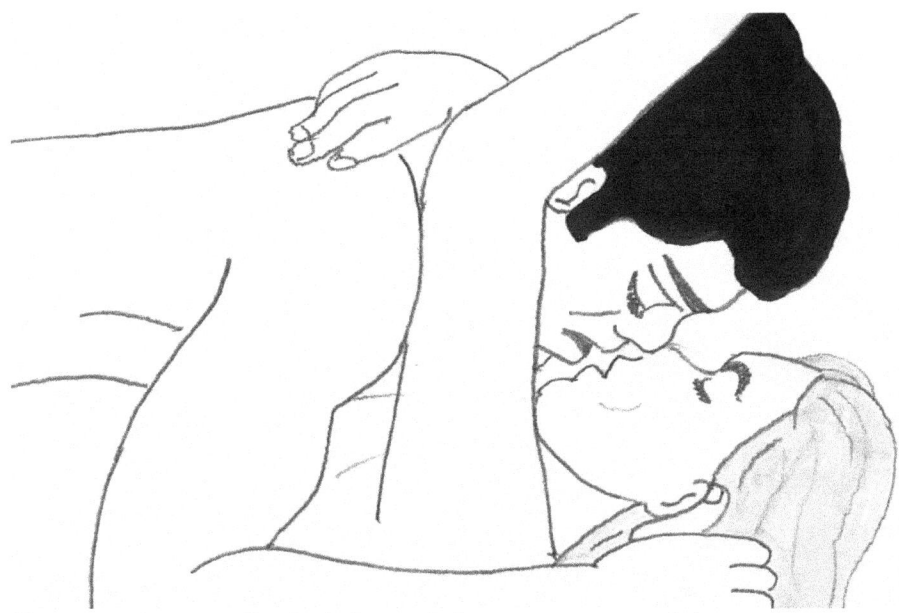

Eve woke to find Adam lying on top of her. He was heavier and stronger and she was at his mercy. Adam lay still. What was he thinking? She too remained still with his weight upon her.

Adam sensed that Eve was awake. 'There's an elephant in the room.'

Eve pushed him off her. 'Well I'm sorry Adam, but I'm not entirely sure that you're the one.'

'What are you talking about? Look, over there.'

An elephant had stepped over a collapsed wall and its trunk that was exploring the room grabbed Adam between the legs.

Unable to contain herself, Eve burst out laughing as Adam pushed the elephant's trunk away and turned his back on her.

'I sense a lot of anger in you,' she said, 'would you like to talk about it?'

'Not as much as you so go to sleep.'

Adam was soon snoring and Eve used what little moonlight filtered through the roof to look at his body. At the back of her mind was the thought that he might have found someone else. Adam rolled onto his back and as she watched the rise and fall of his chest she decided to count his ribs to put her mind at rest. Her fingers carefully prodded his chest to confirm that only one rib was missing, and with her thirst for knowledge driving her on, Eve's fingers began to move further down his body.

In Adam's nightmare, more of his ribs were being removed by the creator. 'Get your hands off me!' he yelled as he woke up.

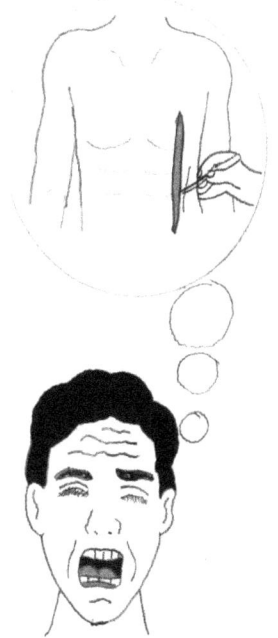

Eve snatched her hand back to her side.

'Oh, it's you,' he mumbled, rubbing the sleep out of his eyes. 'I thought it was someone else.'

Eve began to cry. 'I knew it! You're cheating on me!'

Adam stared at the unfathomable woman before him. 'Now you're being silly. Have you ever seen me look at another woman? I had a bad dream, that's all. I felt fingers on my chest and thought that the creator was taking more ribs. Get some beauty sleep.'

Eve did not know how to take that. 'Are you saying that I'm ugly?'

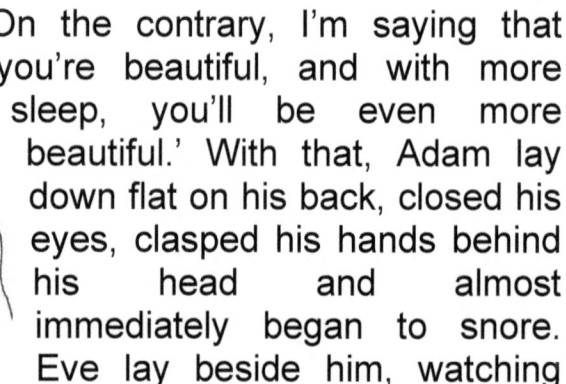

'On the contrary, I'm saying that you're beautiful, and with more sleep, you'll be even more beautiful.' With that, Adam lay down flat on his back, closed his eyes, clasped his hands behind his head and almost immediately began to snore. Eve lay beside him, watching and waiting. Although she took comfort from this rare compliment, she fully expected there would be an ulterior motive and she didn't have long to wait. Adam's whisper broke the silence. 'I'm nearly asleep now, feel free to have another grope. You know you want to.'

Eve turned away from him deep in thought. How much longer could she go on fighting her feelings for him? Another week? Another day? Another hour?

Adam soon fell asleep but Eve could not. The knowledge that she would one day lay an egg scared her and it didn't help that the father would be Adam.

CHAPTER 6

THE

FIRST KISS

Rays of sunlight penetrating his poorly made man-cave cast dancing shadows across Eve's shoulders. Adam longed to run his fingers through her blonde hair, to feel the warmth of her body next to his, to show his love for her. Eve had become increasingly aware of him beside her, of the feel of his bare chest against her, of the steady reassuring beat of his heart. She longed for his arms to encircle her to soothe away her fears so that she could show him how much she cared. Her heart soared when his strong arms wrapped securely around her and when he kissed her on the lips, she did not push him away.

'Oh, baby,' he sighed. 'You don't know how badly I've wanted to kiss you. It's been hell for me all week...'

Using both hands, she pushed him away and sat up. 'So, this is not about making me happy, this is you using me just to make you feel better.'

'I was hoping that it would make you feel better too, but now that you've made your feelings clear and I know where I stand, I won't bother you again.'

Eve was angry and confused; conflicting emotions tumbled around inside her. Why did I open my big mouth? Why didn't I let nature take its course?

'I've got an idea,' said Adam. 'Let's become friends with benefits.'

'Friends with benefits? What exactly do you mean, friends with benefits?'

'We'll get more work done if we work apart. If I need you, I'll give you a call.'

Eve shrugged. 'Fine, have it your way.'

Adam moved outside, picked up a stick and threw it for Patch who quickly returned to his master's side with stick in mouth, his tail making it clear that he was happy. 'It's a pity you don't have a tail,' he shouted over his shoulder, 'then I'd be able to tell what mood you were in. I'll see you later.'

'Missing you already,' Eve shouted as he quickly put distance between them.

Needing a new, stronger man-cave in a better location, Adam set off and continued to moan about Eve to his dog. 'She even talks in her sleep, Patch. Can you believe it? And sometimes, when she's asleep she makes loud noises that smell real bad. I think it's because she eats too much fruit,' and to add to his miserable day, he stubbed his toe on a large rock.

The idea to build a stone man-cave well away from banana trees gave him new purpose. He sat on a rock and with a stick drew a picture of his dream house in the dirt. He gathered rocks for the walls throughout the day and used branches for the roof instead of banana leaves, leaving a small gap in one wall and for the entrance, just wide enough for humans or dogs but too narrow for sheep or elephants; there would be no animal droppings in this house. To the left of his narrow doorway, he placed two smooth square rocks against the outer wall, filled the gap between them with straw and sat down resting his arms on the stones to try out his new armchair for size. Perfect. After placing a handful of nuts on the arm of his chair, Adam made a roof using more branches and although there were several holes, he didn't mind because he preferred to fall asleep counting stars rather than sheep.

Satisfied with his construction, Adam set off to find Patch who had gone missing. Without his dog, Adam was completely lost and through field after field he trudged following the sparkling blue of the river that snaked through the middle of the valley. 'PATCH!' he shouted, his voice echoing through the valley before him. 'PATCH! HERE BOY!' A flock of white birds disturbed by his shouting squawked loudly as they took flight and movement in the undergrowth raised Adam's spirits. 'Patch, is that you?'

The serpent slithered into view, 'Are you lossst? Your dog isss thisss way.'

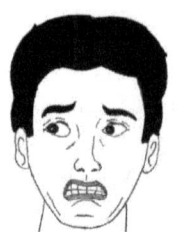

Adam followed the shiny green scales deeper and deeper into the valley. 'This is very kind of you Mr Snake, I'm sorry that my dog attacked you the other day, I don't know what came over him.'

'That'sss alright,' hissed the cunning snake as it led Adam into a carefully prepared trap, 'thisss is a ssshortcut I found yesssterday.'

They stood at a clearing in the middle of an orchard with one path blocked by apples and leaves. The snake burrowed through the fruit and leaves and beckoned Adam to follow. 'Thisss way,' hissed the snake knowing that even the slightest touch of one of the apples would be enough to open Adam's eyes to good and evil, 'Just pusssh everything to the ssside and follow me.'

Adam stepped forward. 'Lead the way my friend. I'm right behind you.'

THE FIRST BATTLE OF THE SEXES

Although a short distance away, the sound of the hissing serpent reached Patches acute hearing and he raced into the orchard, his low growl intensifying into a roar befitting an angry lion which forced the crafty snake to slither out of sight. Patch's eyes remained fixed on the undergrowth, ready to pounce if the snake dared to return.

Adam had never seen his dog act so aggressively. 'Patch, the snake was just bringing me to you, you should not be so jealous, you're a bad dog!' Patch continued to guard his master until Adam gave the order, 'let's go home.'

Late in the afternoon, Eve found Adam's impressive newly-built stone man-cave which was big enough for two, and whilst she waited for him to return, she practised throwing coconuts so that the next time he annoyed her, she wouldn't miss. One coconut hit the stone wall and split in two to reveal coconut milk, yet another new discovery. Hungry and thirsty, Eve scoffed some nuts that lay on a large flat stone and washed them down with coconut milk. 'Why are men so untidy?' she mumbled, sweeping up the straw and sticks that in her opinion littered the place.

Adam's gaze at last fell onto his newly constructed home and he patted his dog's head. 'Good boy, I don't know how you found it but good boy, well done. Now we can rest in peace and quiet.'

Eve appeared in the doorway. 'And what time do you call this?'

Adam's shoulders slumped. 'What kind of welcome home is that?'

'What do you expect? You go off doing God knows what; you say you're gonna call, but you don't.' She was building up a head of steam and Adam had learned the hard way not to interrupt her. 'Where have you been? What took you so long?'

Adam decided honesty was best. 'I got lost.'

'What is it with men? Why don't you ask for directions?' Adam hung his head low, deciding not to mention the snake, and Eve continued to make her point. 'Perhaps you should have befriended a homing pigeon instead of a dog.'

'He's not just a dog, he's my BFFF, Best Furry Friend Forever.' Adam looked at the empty space where Patch's sticks should have been, 'and where are his sticks?' Adam turned to his armchair, 'and where is the moss from my armchair?'

'I've tidied up, I thought you'd be pleased.'

Adam looked at the empty arm of his armchair, 'and where are my nuts?'

'If you don't know by now,' she said with a smile, 'it's no wonder that we're not populating the world.'

Adams comfortable home had been transformed, and he was not pleased.

'If you must know, housework made me hungry so I ate your nuts but if I tell you a secret, will you promise to keep it to yourself?' Adam nodded so Eve held out half a coconut with milk inside. 'I bet you never knew that coconuts contained delicious milk.'

Adam swiped the half coconut out of her hand and Patch, thinking this was a new game, pounced on it. 'PATCH, LEAVE!' ordered Adam, and Patch, not liking this new game, slunk away with his tail between his legs. 'Great, now you've upset my dog, you idiot.'

THE FIRST BATTLE OF THE SEXES

'You're the idiot,' snapped Eve.

'No I'm not, didn't I name all the animals?'

'Yeah, great job, except that a bald eagle isn't bald, a sea horse isn't a horse, a guinea pig isn't a pig, a dragonfly isn't a dragon or a fly, and why did you call the big ugly animal a hippopotamus?'

'Because woman was taken.'

Eve picked up another coconut and although Adam turned to run, her aim was straight and true and the coconut bounced off the back of his head.

CHAPTER 7

THE ARGUMENTS CONTINUE

Adam tried to ease the tension. 'Let's not cry over spilt milk - thank you for tidying up.' A spark of hope ignited in Eve's heart, perhaps they could learn to get along after all? 'Only next time you move any of my possessions,' he continued, 'ask my permission because I was created first.'

They looked at each other and Adam waited for her to drop her eyes, but she held his stare. 'Your trouble is, you think you're God's gift to women – and I can assure you that you're not.'

Adam appealed to the heavens. 'Excuse me Mr Creator, why are women so irritable?'

Eve answered for him. 'Women are more irritable than men because men are more irritating.'

Adam had no appetite to continue fighting. 'It's late, it's dark and we're both tired. Do you want to stay here tonight? There's plenty of room?'

'For a moment there,' Eve said, 'it sounded like you cared.'

'Of course I care. It's my duty to keep you safe.'

'Is that how you see me, as a duty?'

'What I'm trying to say, if you would only listen, is that I do care about you.'

Adam looked as if he were about to say something more, but Eve put her fingers to her ears because she was in no frame of mind to listen. She was furious, furious at the surge of joy she'd felt when she saw him and furious at him because he wasn't even remotely pleased to see her. She bit her lip, remembering his comment about it being 'his duty' to look after her. She could *never* be interested in a man like that. Despite herself, Eve felt a tiny thrill shoot through her. Did that mean that he had begun to have feelings for her, even if it was not yet love? No matter how hard she tried to remain calm, her heart soared at the thought. Propped up on one elbow beside him, Eve wrestled with her emotions. Was it possible that Adam had fallen in love with her as she had him?

Adam lay flat on his back exhausted from a day's hard work and dreamed of one day filling Eve with his tadpoles.

Because he was more focussed on his dog and building the perfect man-cave, women, romance and lovemaking remained a complete mystery to him.

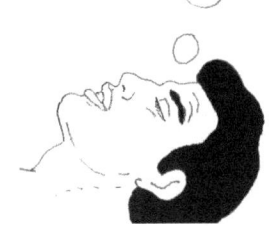

Eve was first to wake up and deciding that gaining more knowledge was preferable to more arguments, she soon found herself running through pine trees into a meadow. A honey bee landed on her nose and they studied each other closely until the honey bee took flight. Determined to put Adam out of her mind, Eve skipped along behind the honey bee to its home, a hollowed-out tree trunk about head high. Because Eve was interested in nature, her brain provided all the information for her to understand and appreciate the uniformed hexagonal holes in the honeycomb and the work-rate of the bees as they built it larger. Because she had not yet fully focussed on Adam, man remained a complete mystery to her; an annoying, attractive, mystery.

To move creation along, the creator instilled in Adam's mind the desire to apologise and Adam set off in search of Eve. Much to his amusement, he found her sitting cross-legged by the river with her eyes closed. 'What are you doing?'

Eve opened her eyes and Adam's smug face came into focus. 'What do you want?'

Adam asked again. 'What are you doing?'

'Yoga; it's a form of relaxation, a way of connecting to your inner self.'

'Well, I suppose it's better than sitting around doing nothing. Can you teach me to do yoga?'

'That depends, how flexible are you?'

'I'm free today and tomorrow.' The lead that Adam had made from a piece of vine and tied around his waist had worked loose so he tightened it.

'What's that?' said Eve pointing.

Adam covered his dangly thing. 'I think you know what that is.'

'I'm talking about the vine around your waist.'

'Oh, this,' he said, putting his hand through a loop at one end. 'It's a lead for my dog if I ever find him, would you like to try it?'

'You'd like that, wouldn't you, to have me on a lead and under your control.'

Adam tried hard not to smile at the thought.

The creator gave Adam another mental reminder to apologise. 'I'm sorry for treating you badly,' Adam said, 'I'm going for a wash in the river, would you care to join me?'

Unsure whether to accept his half-hearted apology, Eve still had reservations. 'Is this another one of your tricks?'

'No tricks, I promise.'

Although eager to join this new caring Adam, Eve held back. 'You carry on and I'll think about it.'

After waiting a short time so as not to appear too keen, Eve was delighted to arrive at the river to find Adam still there and without his dog. Perhaps he'll focus on me for a change she thought as she slid into the water with exquisite grace, her head held high and her eyes looking straight ahead, and Adam's heart thudded inside his chest at the sight of her. He reached out when she stumbled, caught her in his arms and pulled her close. Eve wondered if it was human to need to be held, to need to be close to another living body – but should she give in to that need? It might become a habit, she might come to need it, to need him. He might be gentle and kind now but he wasn't when they first met, so what did that tell her about him? That he was bossy and selfish, hardly Mister Right.

The creator whispered to Eve, *'Submit to him, everything will be just fine.'*

Adam stood behind her and massaged her shoulders. 'I love our mornings at the river.'

Eve considered her options. She had been ready to admit for some time now that she had feelings for him, and those feelings now ran wildly through her; but did he feel the same way? Did he even have any feelings for her at all? If only he would say 'I love you.' If only he felt half of the affection that she felt for him, life could be so much sweeter. She wasn't afraid of Adam, but she had too much to lose if she weakened. Her voice rose as she trembled with a mixture of emotions. 'Please remove your hands from my shoulders; I'm quite capable of washing myself.'

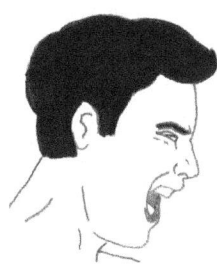

'Suit yourself,' he said with a shrug, and his eyes turn cold. In some ways, he felt relieved that the moment had passed because he hadn't a clue what to do next.

'*Romance,*' whispered the creator. '*She needs romance.*'

Adam followed the creator's instructions. 'Eve, will you be my valentine?'

Valentine? Was it possible that he was actually serious? 'Are you asking me out on a date?'

'Y-y-yes,' Adam stuttered rolling his eyes skyward hoping for further instructions, but none came.

'What's the dress code?'

'It's a come-as-you-are housewarming party at my place.'

They agreed to meet mid-afternoon and headed off in opposite directions to get ready.

CHAPTER 8

DATE NIGHT

With her blonde hair dancing crazily in the breeze, Eve skipped down to the waterfall and had a long shower before using her reflection in the river to tweak her hair several times with a porcupine quill. After deciding that she needed a nice outfit, she found some shiny fig leaves and made herself a skirt and top, then she rubbed numerous plants and herbs between her fingers in the meadow until she found a perfume that she liked and she put on enough eye make up to confuse a panda. After inserting a red flower into her hair and dabbing her new perfume behind her ears, she put on her new clothes and returned to the river to check her reflection one last time. Then she blew herself a kiss, turned left and right to make sure her outfit looked good from every angle and set off for her date.

To prepare for his date, Adam searched for his missing dog, picked some wild flowers and with plenty of time before his date lay down and slept for a while. Waking from his nap during which he had rolled onto the wild flowers he had picked for Eve, Adam stretched, ran his fingers through his hair, picked up the squashed flowers and returned home for his date.

74

On her way to Adam's new house, a slurping noise attracted Eve's attention. She crept into a nearby field to see spring lambs suckling on their mother's teats. The ewe lay on her side with a look of complete contentment as her teats were being suckled. Anticipating the joy and satisfaction of motherhood, Eve increased her pace and reached the perimeter wall of Adam's house before pausing to take a deep breath.

Adam appeared in the doorway, hands behind his back. 'You're late.'

Eve's shoulders slumped; she had really begun to believe she and Adam could be happy together, that it wasn't just an impossible dream. Who was she trying to kid? 'Sorry I'm late.' Eve stepped nervously inside, wondering if he's tidied up from the night before, he hadn't. Adam stood before her; his dark curly hair scrunched up as if he'd been dragged through a hedge backwards. He hadn't noticed her hair, her clothes, her eye shadow or her perfume, and he had obviously made no effort at all.

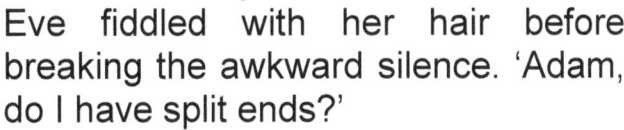

Eve fiddled with her hair before breaking the awkward silence. 'Adam, do I have split ends?'

Adam carefully examined the ends of her fingers. 'I don't think so.'

THE FIRST BATTLE OF THE SEXES

A woman likes compliments, reminded the creator.

Adam inhaled Eve's perfume. 'You smell nice.'

That's more like it, thought the creator, until Adam continued with: 'Have you been jogging?'

Eve scowled. 'That's not very romantic.'

'I'm sorry Eve; it's just that when I'm nervous, I say the wrong thing. Look, will you close your eyes?'

Eve shook her head. 'I can't look if I close my eyes.'

'Now who's not being romantic?'

'Point taken,' said Eve closing her eyes. Her lips were inches from his and her body was inches from his powerful arms that for some reason were behind his back.

'Now hold out your hands, I've got a present for you.'

Eve held out her hands in anticipation.

From behind his back, Adam produced the bunch of squashed flowers and placed them in her hands. 'Surprise!'

Eve opened her eyes, threw the squashed flowers

and the flower in her hair onto the floor. 'Flowers? We live in the Garden of Eden and you bring me flowers? No wonder you have no friends.'

'Hark who's talking. I found your face book and you only have one friend – me!'

'Well that's one more than you've got,' Eve fumed, 'because I hate you!' She ran from the house. What she wanted was romance and compliments not criticism and childish behaviour. Adam, she decided, did not have a romantic bone in his body.

In an effort to wash Adam from her mind, Eve ran to the river, but she was not alone for long. From the corner of her eye she saw him approaching. He was the most annoying man that she had ever met so why on earth should she feel this quiver of sensual attraction whenever she saw him? She hoped that he

wasn't aware of her secret feelings but something in those sparkling blue eyes made her uneasily suspect that he was. What was he doing here if he disliked her so much?

Adam entered the water and pressed up against her. At his touch, Eve's breath caught in her throat, and then a low moan escaped from her lips. His gaze lowered to her mouth and she unconsciously moistened her lips. His breath quickened but she was determined not to respond in any way so she stood rigidly in the circle of his arms. Her eyes were huge as she looked up at him. Why was he  looking at her like that? For a moment their glances held, and then he leaned forward and kissed her. She saw something in his glance that made her blush. 'And what was that for?'

Tell her you love her, whispered the creator.

Reluctant to say the 'L' word, Adam said, 'Doesn't it make sense to experiment?'

Eve studied his deep blue eyes and she began to wish that he hadn't kissed her. Everything was becoming far too complicated. 'Have you finished experimenting with me now?'

Disappointed at her lack of response, Adam continued to wash himself. 'Yes, I've finished now thank you.'

Eve couldn't speak for crying. It felt as if her heart was full of love and sorrow at the same time. 'Is that all I am to you, an experiment?' Although she'd tried to minimize the effects of his lips against hers, Eve could not deny that it felt good and right and she wanted more, yet confusion crushed those feelings.

'I'm going to find my dog,' Adam said and headed downstream.

Left alone, Eve dressed and stared down the lonely pathway of her future. She knew that if she had given herself to Adam it would have become real, but if she kept herself for herself it would be nothing, and what she discovered later that afternoon sent a cold shiver down her spine. It was an egg, a pain-fully large egg. A large bird covered in brown feathers ran towards her with large wings flapping wildly. 'Relax, Mrs Ostrich,' Eve shouted, realising that the bird, despite the speed of her legs and the size of her wings, would never actually fly. 'I mean you and your egg no harm.' Eve's hands went to her special place and she swallowed hard, wondering just how painful it would be to lay Adam's egg. The decision was made, Eve vowed to remain a virgin forever.

Downstream, Adam picked up a stick. 'It's time you learned to swim.' Patch who had just returned assumed the position, crouching low ready to sprint after it. 'Fetch,' Adam shouted as he threw the stick and Patch was after it in a flash. For a moment, the dog was almost underneath it but as the stick splashed into the river, Patch skidded to a halt just a few inches from the bank and turned to his master with a look that said, "Do I look that stupid?"

Although his plan hadn't worked, Adam watched the stick float downstream and another construction project came to mind, one that could put a great

distance between himself and the argumentative and emotional woman he could leave behind. He gathered and bound several thick logs of similar lengths together with vines, made the world's first raft, dragged it into the water and called his dog. 'Patch, here boy.'

Patch nervously approached his master only to have his lead tied tightly around his neck. Adam stepped onto his new wooden structure and pulled and pulled on the lead. Patch had two choices: die of strangulation or get on board. Reluctantly, Patch joined his master and they floated gently downstream. Adam had one thought in his mind, to get as far away from Eve as possible.

CHAPTER 9

DIVINE

INTERVENTION

The creator looked down on all he had made and saw that it was good. Creation was going to plan except for one minor detail. Adam preferred to spend time with his dog because Eve was far too emotional and argumentative; and Eve, having seen the size of an ostrich egg and thinking that she would have to lay a similar sized egg for Adam, had vowed to remain a virgin forever.

There was only one solution to the Adam and Eve problem, the creator would have to give his children the talk that all parents dread: he would have to explain to them the facts of life.

THE FIRST BATTLE OF THE SEXES

Deciding to begin with Adam, the creator gently blew the raft ashore and Patch ran into the nearby forest to relieve himself.

Adam looked to the heavens. 'Why did you do that?'

Nervously, the creator began. *'We need to talk about Eve, what have you learned about her so far?'*

'If she's not arguing and remains silent, she's asleep.'

'We need to have a serious talk son.'

'Wow,' said Adam, 'I'd never thought of you as my father, only as my creator, which would you prefer?'

'Father will be fine. Let's talk about the birds and the bees.'

'OK dad, I understand about them, it's women that I don't understand.'

'That's because women are made differently to men.'

'I had noticed, I particularly like her pair of ...'

'What I'm trying to say, Adam,' interrupted the creator, *'is that women are made differently physically and they also think differently.'*

83

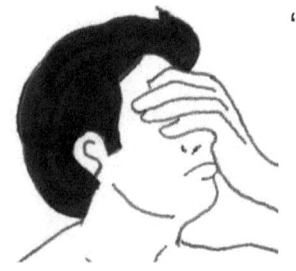

'Tell me about it! Eve says that I don't listen to her, or something like that.'

The creator smiled. *'Adam, she is correct, you don't listen to her.'*

'Tell me, if a man is standing in the middle of an orchard and says something, and there is no woman around to hear him, is he still wrong?'

'Adam, what a woman wants to hear are compliments.'

'I told her she was beautiful?'

'Yes, but then you followed with "almost as beautiful as my dog."'

'But my dog *is* beautiful! One minute Eve's warm, the next minute she's cold; women should come with instructions.'

'Would you read them?'

'Of course not, but that's not the point.'

'Eve needs romance, you need to show her your romantic side.'

Adam knew that he had a left side and a right side, but a romantic side? *'Adam,' continued the creator, 'you need to make Eve feel special. Women need compliments and presents.'*

'But that costs money. Can you increase my pocket money?'

'I don't give you any pocket money.'

'Exactly! What kind of father are you?'

The creator sighed; the talk was not going well. *'Adam, calm down and listen to me, I want you to do what the other animals are doing.'*

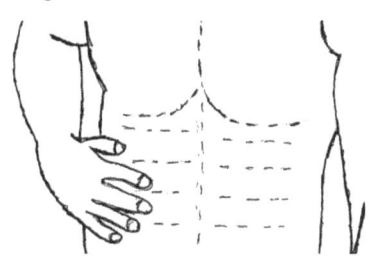

'What's that, climb trees, lay eggs, eat grass, swim? At least give me a clue.'

'Adam, I want you and Eve to multiply.'

'I already know how to multiply. Two times two is four, 12 times 12 is – lots.'

The creator took a deep breath. *'Adam, I think you know what I want. I want you to sleep with her.'*

'But she farts in her sleep.'

'Adam, I want you and Eve to make babies and this is something that you have to do together.'

Adam felt his ribcage. "Can't you make us some babies? I don't mind a little pain and I've still got plenty of ribs.'

'Adam, I will not be removing any of your ribs and I can assure you that when you and Eve make babies there will be no pain, only pleasure.'

'Are you sure about that? How many times have you made babies?'

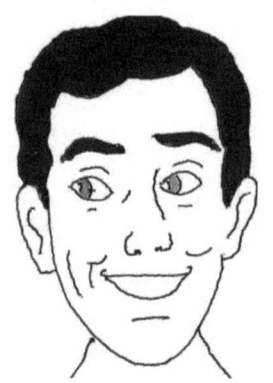

'Your first time will be my first time.'

'If I do sleep with Eve, will you be watching if we – you know – try to do it?'

'Of course not! I'll avert my eyes.'

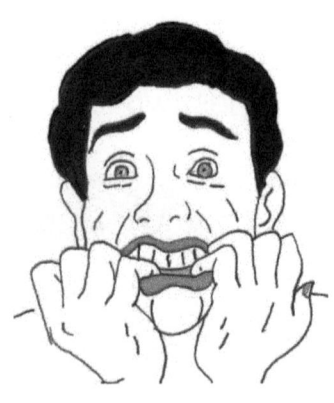

'Promise?'

'I promise, and Adam…'

'Yes?'

'I'll help you if you get stuck.'

Adam frowned. 'Is there a chance that I might get stuck?'

The creator regretted his choice of words. *'Adam, if you are tender, gentle and loving, everything will turn out just fine.'*

Adam looked down at his dangly thing. 'Come on,' he said. 'We have a job to do.'

The creator found Eve who was still thinking about the ostrich egg.

'Eve, it's time we had a little chat about the birds and the bees.'

'I understand that birds lay eggs and buzzing bees make honey, it's men that I don't understand.'

'That's because men are made differently.'

'Oh, yes, I had noticed. I particularly like that willie you gave Adam; did you see the elephant grab it the other night? It was so funny.'

'Yes, it was funny,' the creator agreed.

'Do you watch us all of the time?'

'Not always my child.'

'Wow,' said a startled Eve. 'I never thought of you as my father, more that you were my creator. What should I call you, father or creator?'

'Father will be just fine.'

'Father, please help me to understand men.'

87

THE FIRST BATTLE OF THE SEXES

'What have you learned about man so far?'

'Man was created first and he is stronger, but he has no feelings and no emotional bones in his body.'

'Adam does have feelings but because men think differently to women, they tend to hide their emotions.'

'His emotions are clear about his dog and what he has built, but he only sees me as a nuisance.'

'Just like you, Adam needs compliments and presents.'

'In that case, I need more pocket money.'

'But I don't give you any?.'

'Exactly! What kind of father are you?'

'A loving one who has given you the perfect climate, vegetables, fruits and flowers of all kinds, and of course Adam.'

'In the future, more women will graduate college than men, they will earn more than their spouses and they will still do most of the parenting and housework. Tell me again why I need him?'

'Eve, I want you and Adam to be fruitful and multiply.'

'I already eat lots of fruit and I know how to multiply on my own, so why do I need him?'

'If you sleep with Adam, you can make babies together.'

'But I don't trust him.'

'Why ever not?'

'Well, for a start, he never looks me straight in the eye.'

'I think you'll find that is because of the way I designed your body.'

'And he snores.'

'Eve, it is important that you sleep with Adam.'

'But when I sleep with him, he pokes me in the back with his willie.'

'When he does that Eve, you need to turn over.'

'Is that what Mrs Creator does?'

The creator hesitated. *'There is no Mrs Creator.'*

Eve thought about the ostrich egg. 'Can't you just take a few of Adam's ribs and make us some children? It would be a lot less painful for me.'

'Eve, I want you to trust me. You will not have to lay an extra-large egg like the one you discovered, you just need to submit to Adam and let him make love to you.'

Eve began to warm to the idea. 'Father, will you be watching if I let him?'

'Of course not my child, I will avert my eyes.'

'Promise?'

'I promise, and Eve…'

'Yes father?'

'I'll help you if you get stuck.'

'Is there a chance we might get stuck together?'

The creator again regretted his choice of words. *'Neither of you will get physically stuck and there will be no pain, only pleasure.'*

'Are you telling me that from experience?'

The creator took a deep breath. 'I've never actually done it, Eve, your first time will be my first time.'

'I wish Adam was kind, considerate and patient like you father.'

'My child, although Adam does not show his feelings very often, he does love you and is making his way down to the river hoping to find you there.'

CHAPTER 10

'OH - MY - GOD!'

With his dog nowhere to be found, Adam turned his attention to finding Eve and with a new urgency he strode quickly down to the river and joined her in the water. Eve's heart hammered against his ribs as their eyes met and he pulled her close. Something odd seemed to be happening inside her; a kind of weakening of the stomach muscles, a feeling that her body was no longer entirely her own.

'I'm scared,' she whispered, tracing circles with her fingers on his broad chest, 'but I want you to take me.' Eve flashed a smile so angelic, for a moment Adam thought he heard harps playing.

Fighting the urge to yell with relief, he wanted to be sure. 'Take you where?'

Her arms stole up around his neck and she moved closer, wanting to feel every inch of his skin against hers. 'Take me to a place I've never been before.'

Adam thought hard. 'Have you ever been on a raft?'

Eve's head tilted to one side, her long wet hair falling over one shoulder as she encouraged him. 'Make love to me Adam, please, make love to me.'

Adam hesitated. 'I'm nervous.'

'Are they first time nerves?'

'No, I've been nervous lots of times.'

Using telepathy, the creator urged them on and crossed his fingers behind his robe.

Adam helped Eve out of the water and they lay side-by-side on the grass in the warmth of the sun. His hands pressed into her back, his fingers splayed, each

digit sending waves of desire through her body. Her spirit sang as he rolled on top of her and when his lips came down on hers any resistance melted away. She laced her fingers through his hair, her body pressing hard against his. It was wonderful for her when he responded. This was no time to be coy, she decided, obeying the urges that were overriding her mind and body. The surface of her skin tingled under his kisses, stirring her very blood and pushing her to a more intense state of excitement. 'Please,' she whispered, her eyes anxiously encouraging him. 'Please,' she panted, 'don't stop.'

Their creator watched with bated breath as his plan headed towards fruition.

A sense of wonder filled Adam's mind. Something unbelievable was happening, a scattering of his senses and then his world exploded. He didn't understand and he didn't care, he just didn't want this moment to end as warmth flooded through him and tadpoles flooded out.

'OH – MY – GOD!' exalted Adam.

'OH – MY – GOD!' exalted Eve.

'OH – MY – GOD!' exalted the creator.

Adam nipped her earlobe gently, his slowing breath warm against her skin sending shivers through her and she felt more cherished than at any time in her life. At last, she felt whole. Adam rolled onto his back pulling her into the cradle of his arms and they both bathed in the warm glow of satisfaction.

Later, they strolled quietly back to Adam's man-cave hand-in-hand and once inside, he lowered her to the ground and as their lips met, every cell and nerve in his body tingled. Eve also became caught up in the intensity of her feelings, everything  centred on her need to touch Adam, to be touched in return, to be loved. She slipped her tongue into his mouth. 'Love me again,' she moaned into his mouth.

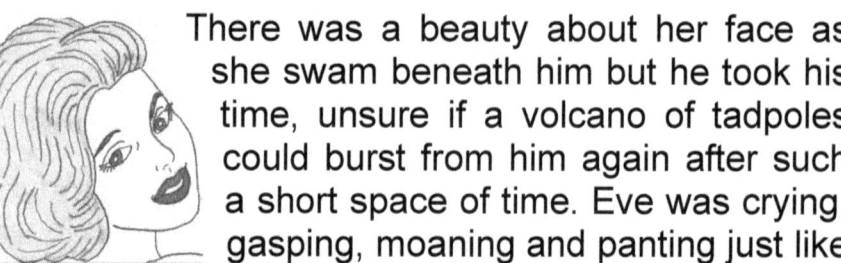 There was a beauty about her face as she swam beneath him but he took his time, unsure if a volcano of tadpoles could burst from him again after such a short space of time. Eve was crying, gasping, moaning and panting just like him as she urged him on and for a second time, tadpoles flooded out of Adam and they both cried out as one, 'OH – MY – GOD!'

Waking first, Adam turned to see Eve lying on her back alongside him, a lock of hair covering one of her eyes. A beam of sunlight filtered through his man-cave roof and reflected off Eve's pure white skin. Propping himself 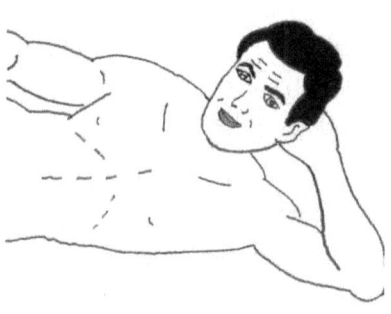 up on one elbow, Adam watched the slow rise and fall of her breasts for a while before walking outside. At the sight of what looked like a bone, Patch wagged his tail in anticipation that sooner or later, his master would stop teasing him and throw it, but as Adam's body-part drooped, so did Patch's ears.

Waking up alone, Eve felt cold and sick inside. The fact that he hadn't hung around for more, she thought glumly, obviously meant that she hadn't lived up to his expectations. Why else would he abandon her? Maybe it was a mistake to trust any man, she decided, as fear of the  unknown started to creep through her. Then she heard Adam's voice outside, he was talking to the creator. She moved to the doorway to listen.

'You were right,' Adam said with a huge smile plastered across his face. 'There was no pain, only great pleasure and I'm not really missing that rib so could you take more ribs and make me some more women?'

Eve pushed past him clutching her broken heart. 'I hate you!' she screamed. 'I knew I shouldn't have trusted you.'

Adam shouted after her. 'I was only joking,

what happened between us was wonderful, please come back.'

Left alone, the afterglow of their coupling quickly faded as fear ran down Adam's spine. Everything had changed. His world, his time alone was over, compromised, this was the start of something new, a new beginning for the two of them. All his life he had been single with just his dog for company, free to do whatever he wanted, but now he was part of a couple.

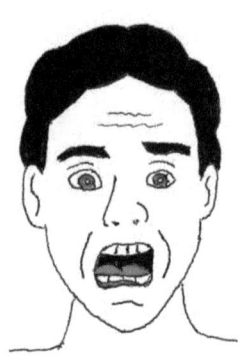

Eve did not hear what Adam had shouted as she pushed past him, all she could remember was that he asked the creator for more women. When she reached the river, her breath caught in her throat as she knelt to take a drink. The blonde hair she recognised and the face that it framed, but this was no longer an innocent woman's reflection, it was one of an experienced woman with a man's tadpoles swimming inside her, tadpoles from a man she could not trust to remain faithful. Not wanting to be found by Adam, Eve sat in the shade of some trees, bit her lip and her eyes filled with tears. She could be a real supportive mate and a lively and passionate lover, if only he would give her a chance.

Waiting patiently for such an opportunity, the crafty snake lowered itself into her view. 'Did the creator really sssay you mussst not eat fruit from any tree?'

'Adam said we must not eat fruit from the tree in the middle of the garden.'

The snake slithered to the ground. 'Well miss, when you eat thisss apple, your eyesss will be opened and you will gain ssso much knowledge, far more than bosssy bootsss.'

Eve's anger and her thirst for knowledge overpowered her senses.

CHAPTER 11

PARADISE

LOST

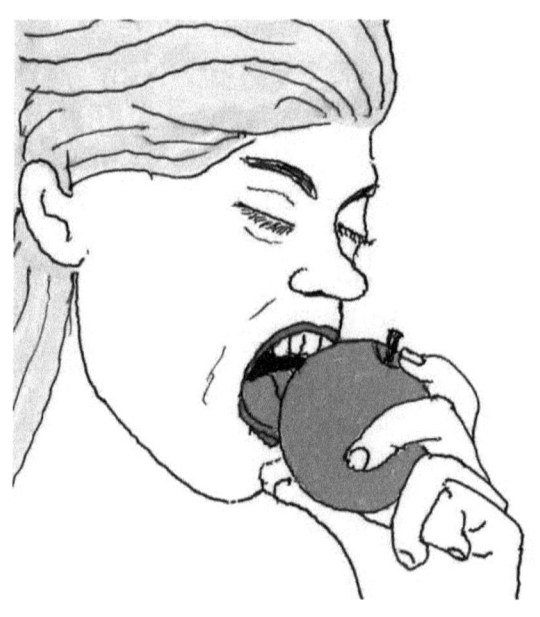

E ve bit into the apple and juice ran down her chin. 'This is good,' she declared, taking more bites. Becoming wiser by the minute, she began to think of ways to become Adam's superior but, fearful of losing him to another female creation, she grabbed another apple. As she rushed to find him, lust and death also entered the world.

As Adam searched for Patch, the clear blue sky began to turn damnation-black and the temperature fell. Different now, the forest concealed murky shadows full of potential danger and through the drizzle of rain that now obscured the beauty and clarity of the once-perfect Garden of Eden, Eve hurried to his side carrying an apple.

Adam held his head in despair. 'What have you done, Eve? What?'

'I ate two apples and they were golden and delicious. Here, taste one, every single person in the world has tried them except you.'

'I can't believe you agreed to the apple terms and conditions without reading them.'

'I know it was stupid and I'm stupid but it's not like the whole world has to know, and it is only an apple, they wouldn't be here if they were poison, and they taste great. Go on taste it, or are you a scaredy cat?'

Adam grabbed the apple. 'I can't believe what you've done, what we've done. This is all your fault.'

Apart from the sound of small creatures scurrying to find a dry place, the orchard remained silent. It was as though all of creation knew that the perfect climate had gone, and no-one knew it more than Adam. 'Patch, here Patch,' he cried into the gathering wind, the sound of his despair muted by the rainfall. He tried again, louder this time. 'PATCH, HERE BOY.'

An eagle, its feathers like the fingers of spread hands, majestically swooped down and in a graceful transformation from flight to murderous attack, its legs dropped, its claws gripped a body of brown fur, and with two or three beats of its powerful wings, the bird of prey soared away with another victim.

Adam looked at Eve and stared at her breasts. Realising that she was naked, Eve tried to cover her breasts with one hand and her private place with the other: 'And you can stop looking at me like that.' Even as the words were slipping out of her mouth, she too saw Adam in a new light, and it was Adam's turn to feel awkward.

His penis that was once just a dangly thing was pointing upwards and he covered it with his hands, worried that his tadpoles might burst out as he desperately tried to think of something else other than the tiny goosebumps around Eve's nipples. Feeling shame, Adam quickly found a fig leaf big enough to cover himself.

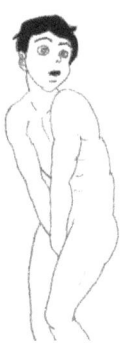

Eve also felt shame so she tried to cover herself with fig leaves, then she tried on maple leaves, oak leaves and beech leaves. 'At least the apple had zero cholesterol,' Eve said deciding finally on the fig leaves which she successfully sewed together so that they could both cover themselves. 'Would you like me to make some clothes for your dog?'

'There's no need, he already wears a fur coat and pants.' (Think about it – Ed).

Every nerve in Adam's body prickled with a sense of danger as he escorted Eve back to his man-cave. 'Stay here,' he ordered using a large stone to partly block the doorway to keep her safe inside. 'I need to go and find my dog, I'll be as quick as I can.'

'Let me come with you,' she pleaded, 'four eyes are better than two.'

'Just do as I say for once. I wear the plants in this family.' Although Eve also wore plants, she let that comment lie. At least he was thinking they were now a family.

At the forest edge, Adam was spellbound and revolted in equal measures and the hairs on the back of his neck rose like the hackles of his dog as fear, a feeling he was unused to, knotted his stomach.

He watched a leopard that stood a short distance away at the edge of thick bushes that fringed the meadow, poised elegantly in skin of black and gold,

long-limbed and small bellied. It moved then, blurring with speed, skimming the ground with the lightest touch with the elegance of a bird swooping to drink whilst continuing in flight, eating up the ground as it hunted down its prey. A howl, or was it a bark, shortly followed. Surely a death cry, the last breath from an animal with little chance of escape, little chance of survival. Man-meat might now be on the menu thought Adam and decided that Eve had been left alone for far too long.

On his return, Adam found some animal skin clothes that had been left outside the man-cave by the creator. 'Leather trousers?' yelled Adam to the storm clouds overhead. 'Haven't I suffered enough?'

Eve had squeezed past the stone in the man-cave entrance to investigate the clothes and modelled a leopard-skin dress. 'Does my bum look big in this?' she asked. Adam's eyes flitted over her in appreciation and Eve blushed. Eve held her sadness just below the surface, her guilt she buried deeper. Now was not the time to let her tears flow, she needed to be strong for Adam, and also for herself. 'Did you find your dog?'

Adam turned his head, his eyes glazed over from staring too long into the distance. 'I'm sorry, what did you say?'

'Did you find your dog?'

'No.'

'Your dog is clever and fearless, look how he protected us from the snake.'

'One more shout,' he said. 'Let me give him one more shout,' and Adam yelled once more into the distance. 'PATCH, HERE BOY!' In the gathering gloom a jackal barked twice and an owl hooted, but his beloved dog was missing presumed dead.

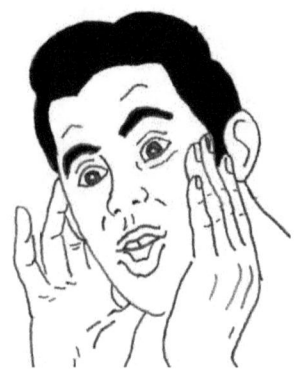

That evening, they lay together back-to-back. Adam cried over the loss of his dog, and Eve cried herself to sleep wishing that one day Adam might learn to love her even half as much as his dog.

CHAPTER 12

EVICTION

The following morning, Adam woke to the sound of panting. 'Eve, what are you doing?' he asked; and as he turned over, a familiar rough wet tongue began to lick his face. 'Eve, look,' he shouted. 'Patch is back and in one piece.' Eve had mixed feelings over Patch's return; pleased that Adam was smiling again and please that the dog survived, but resigned to being second in line for Adam's affections.

After taking his dog for a walk, Adam returned and found a letter by the entrance to his man-cave. 'Eve, we've got a letter from the creator in heaven.'

'A letter from heaven, what is it?'

'It's a tranquil place above the clouds where the creator lives.'

Eve sighed. 'What does the letter say?'

'It's a letter Eve, letters don't say anything.'

Eve snatched it out of Adam's hand and read it. 'O-M-G!'

Adam frowned, 'And what does O-M-G mean?'

'Oh My God, I just used the first letters of the words like you did when you described

Patch as your BFFF – Best Furry Friend Forever.'

'Why do we have a letter from the creator? Have we been forgiven?'

'No. It's a Section 21 notice.'

Adam's stomach muscles tightened. 'What's a Section 21 notice?'

'We're being evicted.'

Adam covered his eyes. 'He can't do that, surely?'

'Well he has,' shouted Eve, throwing the letter on the floor. 'I bet it's because we have a dog.'

'I think you'll find it's nothing to do with my dog, it's probably because you ate the forbidden fruit.'

Eve turned on Adam. 'Don't you go laying the blame at my feet, you ate it as well.'

'And whose fault was that? Yours because you listened to a talking reptile.' Adam put on a squeaky voice. "Oh hello, talking snake, you look honest and trustworthy, what would you like me to do, eat this forbidden apple? Why sure, I'll try anything once."'

Eve's thin lips curved into a smile cold enough to cause frostbite. 'Here we go again. Yes, I made a mistake I admit it, but nobody's perfect.'

'Yeah, well we were, until you took advice from a devious reptile.'

'Do you know what I think?' said Eve. 'I think our landlord planted that tree in the middle of the garden on purpose so that he wouldn't have to refund our deposit.'

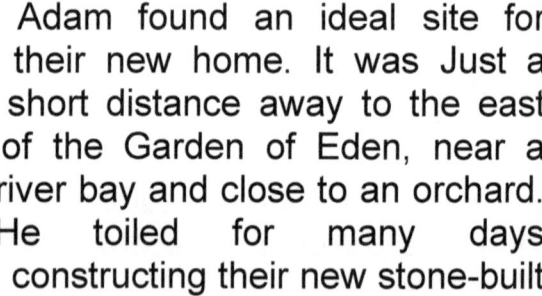

Adam found an ideal site for their new home. It was Just a short distance away to the east of the Garden of Eden, near a river bay and close to an orchard. He toiled for many days constructing their new stone-built home whilst Eve remained in the Garden of Eden packing up their few belongings. To fill the boredom of being left alone each and every day, she studied the animal skin clothes left by the creator and improved her sewing skills to produce lots of clothes, sandals and handbags.

Adam wearily dragged himself home following another long day of construction work but his pace quickened when he saw smoke rising from the Garden of Eden where he found Eve standing before the flames of an open fire. 'What have you done now? Have you been talking to that devious snake again?'

Eve put her hand to her lips. 'If you must know, I was rubbing two wooden sticks together to sharpen my sewing needles and this flame just appeared.'

 'Have you completed a risk assessment? Would you like to run me through your decision tree on this, you being an expert on trees?'

Eve decided to change the subject. 'So how did you do on E-bay?'

'E-bay?'

'East Bay where you have been all day. Is the house ready for us to move in to?'

 'Almost ready, have you gathered up your belongings?' Eve pointed to her growing pile of clothes, sandals and handbags and Adam counted them. 'What's the point of having so many clothes, sandals and handbags?'

'Your trouble Adam is that you only live for the moment whereas I can see beyond the here and now. These accessories are just the beginning, I plan to open a shop and sell my goods on E-bay.'

Adam laughed. 'Who are you going to sell them to? Don't we live in East Bay alone?'

'For now, yes; but we won't be alone for long, the creator told me; and if you don't believe me, go and ask him yourself.'

'I can't do that can I because he doesn't speak to us anymore and we both know why that is don't we.'

CHAPTER 13

MORE

ARGUMENTS

They lay together back-to-back. 'Eve, are you still awake?' whispered Adam before turning over for a cuddle.

Eve pushed his hand away. 'I'm not really in the mood Adam, but it might help if you whisper dirty things in my ear.'

'Kitchen, bedroom, backyard.'

Eve pretended to snore.

Adam tried again to get her in the mood. 'Eve, do you ever fantasise about me?'

'I do Adam, I fantasise about you tidying up occasionally and taking out the trash.'

The following morning at the river, Eve looked at her reflection. 'I feel horrible, I look fat. I look ugly. Adam, I really need you to pay me a compliment.'

'Your eyesight is perfect.'

'I don't need your sarcasm Adam, I'm already feeling blue.'

'Here's some free advice Eve, next time you're feeling blue, stop talking and start breathing.'

'And here's some free advice for you Adam, don't play leapfrog with a unicorn.' Eve put her slate mirror down. 'I don't understand why I'm getting fat, I'm a light eater.'

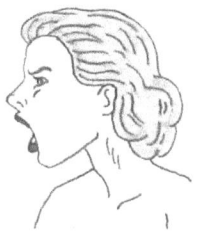

'Exactly, and that's your problem, when it gets light, you eat. Thinking about it, you actually ate us out of our house and home.'

'Yeah, but I got a nice pair of snakeskin boots in the deal. Anyway, I'm certain that a baby is growing inside me, so your comments about my weight aren't fair. '

'Expecting the world to treat you fairly because you are good is like expecting an elephant not to charge because you are a vegetarian.'

'By the way Adam, you forgot my birthday.'

'Actually my dear, you weren't born, so technically, I did not forget your birthday.' Adam decided to leave her then because he knew she was going to weep, and he didn't want to see it.

As she stepped outside and rubbed her aching back, she felt a quiver in her womb as if the sunshine had touched it and made it happy. The baby began to kick continually and Eve had the feeling that it would be just like Adam: obstinate, overbearing, and always wanting its own way.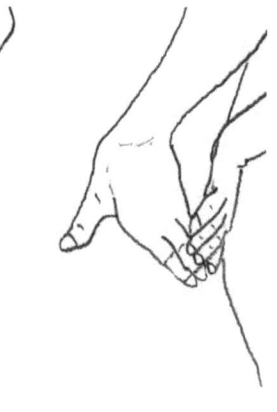

 'Before you clear off for the day, my lord and master, do you want a cooked dinner tonight?'

'Sure, what are my choices?'

'Yes or no.'

'I'll eat anything but sprouts. If only the forbidden fruit had been a sprout ...'

'A sprout is a vegetable, not a fruit,' interrupted Eve.

Adam began to walk away. 'I wish I was in prison, at least then I might be able to finish a sentence.'

Eve shouted after him, 'Don't be late home because I'm going to cook ribs tonight, nothing personal.'

CHAPTER 14

AND THEN THERE WERE THREE

Adam returned home five hours later to find the fire had gone out and no cooked food was ready, not even sprouts. 'Eve, he shouted, 'Where are you, and where's my dinner?'

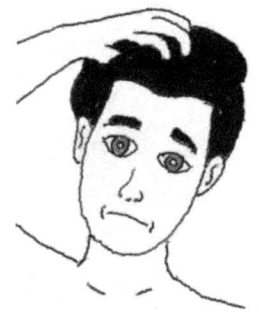

'Ssshh,' she replied from inside, 'or you'll wake the baby.'

Adam peered inside his mancave at something with four legs that had begun to cry. Adam moved closer. 'Where did you find it?'

'I didn't find it Adam, it's the baby we made together, but he has a funny little hole in his belly, like a button. I've never seen anything like it in my life. I'd ask the creator about it, but all we get from him now is the occasional postcard saying, "Garden is fine. Wish you were here."'

Adam looked more closely at the baby and its belly- button. 'He doesn't look like me, are you sure it's mine?' The baby promptly wee'd all over him.

'Of course he's yours, have you ever seen me look at another man?'

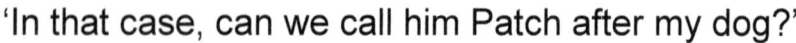

'In that case, can we call him Patch after my dog?'

CHAPTER 15

AND THEN THERE WERE FOUR

'Adam, what do you think we should tell Cain and Abel when they're old enough to understand?'

'I think we should tell them the truth! That I was created first, then you were made from one of my ribs and have been a pain in my side ever since. That we lived in the Garden of Eden until a talking snake told us to eat an apple which made us realise that we were naked which made a voice in the sky kick us out of the Garden of Eden.'

The look on Eve's face made Adam think again. 'On second thoughts Eve, let's just tell them that we met in a bar.'

THE END

ABOUT THE AUTHOR

In my early 20's I tried to write a book based on my experiences of football hooliganism, and because my early reading was Dennis Wheatley books including 'The Devil Rides Out' and 'They Used Dark Forces', I also tried to write a book that included Satanism. Although both books were never completed, creative writing seeds were planted and writing skills awakened.

Those skills lay dormant for over 30 years until I went on a life-changing two week mission to Kenya in 2006. On my return, I turned my diary notes and some Kenya photos into my first book, 'The Accidental Christian'.

Writing changed from a hobby into an obsession and after failing to find a writer's group, I started my own in 2010 and myself and group members began to enter stories (maximum 1,500 words) into the Somerset Short Story Competition (SSSC). In 2011, my first entry made the shortlist, in 2012 I came 3rd, in 2013 I came 2nd and 4th and in 2014 I had stories commended and shortlisted. In 2013 I won a one-act play competition and made the final shortlist of 10 in an international short story competition. In 2016, 'I demand a refund' was one of 12 monologues performed live by the Show of Strength theatre group.

Writing well is not easy but if you have an urge to write, join a writer's group and always carry a notebook and pen to capture ideas and overheard conversations.

*Brian Humphreys is the current chairman of Kenya Hope Charity (Registered number 1173487) and has visited Kenya 14 times on aid missions. Please visit www.kenyahopecharity.org to see videos and details of the work done and plans for the future.

BOOKS BY THE AUTHOR

The following books are all available as Kindle downloads

AFRICAN ADVENTURES OF A BORN-AGAIN ATHEIST

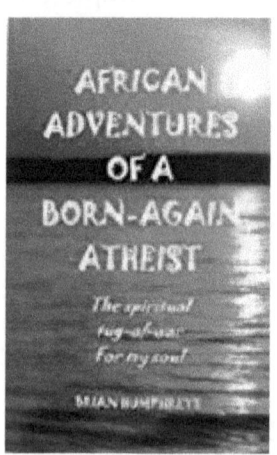

As an atheist, I lived happily in Brian's World until, with the help of minor surgery, God removed the remote control from my left hand and sent me to help the poor in Kenya. God showed me heaven and the devil showed me hell, stretching my belief system to the limit. Christians said I was a tool being used by God. That was extremely harsh. I did my best.

FIFTY COFFEE BREAK SHORT STORIES

From biblical times to the Bristol riots of 2011, each story takes you into a different world, and as you travel in time, so you travel around the world, from darkest Africa to Buckingham Palace, from a Butlins holiday camp to Hell. Stories vary in length from 50 to 2,500 words, so whether you have five minutes or half an hour, pour yourself a drink and enjoy 50 short stories that contain more twists than a Chubby Checker concert.

BUSTER THE TIME-TRAVELLING DOG

Fitted with a faulty time-travel collar, Buster visits The Garden of Eden, the Swinging Sixties, The Ark and the naughty step in Fifty Shades of Geyhound.

The thoughts and opinions expressed in this book are Buster's, and not those of the author who quite likes postmen and ginger cats.

FIFTY SHADES OF SOMERSET

This collection of stories takes you on a unique journey around Somerset. On the surface, Somerset appears to be an idyllic place to live, but if you were to dig a little deeper, you just might unearth the real Somerset.

These saucy, spooky and humorous tales include TEN award-winning stories.